50 British Dinner Dishes for Home

By: Kelly Johnson

Table of Contents

- Fish and chips
- Shepherd's pie
- Cottage pie
- Beef Wellington
- Roast beef and Yorkshire pudding
- Chicken tikka masala
- Bangers and mash
- Toad in the hole
- Beef stew
- Chicken and leek pie
- Cornish pasty
- Steak and kidney pie
- Ploughman's lunch
- Full English breakfast (served for dinner)
- Lancashire hotpot
- Beef and ale stew
- Spaghetti bolognese (British-style)
- Fish pie
- Sausage rolls
- Ragu
- Lamb chops with mint sauce
- Chicken casserole
- Cauliflower cheese
- Sunday roast
- Black pudding and eggs
- Pork pie
- Scampi and chips
- Welsh rarebit
- Scotch eggs
- Sausage and onion casserole
- Grilled kippers
- Bubble and squeak
- Moussaka (British adaptation)
- Chilli con carne
- Hot pot

- Venison stew
- Roast chicken with stuffing
- Steak and chips
- Gammon and eggs
- Toad in the hole with gravy
- Pork roast with apple sauce
- Prawn cocktail (starter but often part of a dinner)
- Chicken pot pie
- Lamb shanks with rosemary
- Shepherd's pie with sweet potato topping
- Chicken and mushroom pie
- Chicken fricassée
- Korma curry (British-style)
- Faggots and peas
- Grilled mackerel

Fish and Chips

Ingredients:

For the fish:

- 4 white fish fillets (cod, haddock, etc.)
- 1 cup (125g) all-purpose flour
- 1 tsp baking powder
- 1/2 tsp salt
- 1/4 tsp ground black pepper
- 1 cup (240ml) cold sparkling water
- Vegetable oil (for frying)

For the chips (fries):

- 4 large potatoes, peeled and cut into thick fries
- Salt to taste

Instructions:

1. Preheat the oil in a deep fryer or large pan to 350°F (175°C).
2. For the chips: Heat oil in a separate pan and fry the potatoes for 4-5 minutes until soft but not browned. Remove and drain on paper towels.
3. For the batter: In a bowl, mix flour, baking powder, salt, and pepper. Gradually whisk in the sparkling water until the batter is smooth and thick.
4. Dip the fish fillets into the batter, then fry them in the hot oil for 5-7 minutes until golden and crispy.
5. Fry the chips again for 3-4 minutes until golden and crispy.
6. Serve the fish and chips with lemon wedges and tartar sauce.

Shepherd's Pie

Ingredients:

- 1 lb (450g) ground lamb
- 1 medium onion, chopped
- 2 cloves garlic, minced
- 1 carrot, diced
- 1/2 cup (120ml) beef or vegetable broth
- 1 tbsp tomato paste
- 1 tsp Worcestershire sauce
- 1 tsp dried thyme
- 4 cups (600g) mashed potatoes (prepared)
- 1/4 cup (60g) frozen peas
- Salt and pepper to taste

Instructions:

1. Preheat oven to 400°F (200°C).
2. In a pan, cook ground lamb over medium heat, breaking it apart with a spoon. Add onion, garlic, and carrot, and cook until softened.
3. Stir in tomato paste, Worcestershire sauce, thyme, and broth. Simmer for 10-15 minutes until the mixture thickens. Add peas, and season with salt and pepper.
4. Transfer the lamb mixture to a baking dish. Top with mashed potatoes, spreading them evenly to cover the filling.
5. Bake for 20-25 minutes until the top is golden and bubbly.

Cottage Pie

Note: Cottage pie is very similar to shepherd's pie but made with ground beef instead of lamb.

Ingredients:

- 1 lb (450g) ground beef
- 1 medium onion, chopped
- 2 cloves garlic, minced
- 1 carrot, diced
- 1/2 cup (120ml) beef broth
- 1 tbsp tomato paste
- 1 tsp Worcestershire sauce
- 1 tsp dried thyme
- 4 cups (600g) mashed potatoes (prepared)
- 1/4 cup (60g) frozen peas
- Salt and pepper to taste

Instructions:

1. Preheat oven to 400°F (200°C).
2. Cook ground beef in a pan over medium heat, breaking it apart. Add onion, garlic, and carrot, and cook until softened.
3. Stir in tomato paste, Worcestershire sauce, thyme, and broth. Simmer for 10-15 minutes until thickened. Add peas, and season with salt and pepper.
4. Transfer the beef mixture to a baking dish and top with mashed potatoes.
5. Bake for 20-25 minutes until the top is golden and bubbly.

Beef Wellington

Ingredients:

- 2 lb (900g) beef tenderloin
- 2 tbsp olive oil
- 2 tbsp Dijon mustard
- 1 lb (450g) mushrooms, finely chopped
- 2 tbsp unsalted butter
- 1/4 cup (60ml) brandy (optional)
- 1 package puff pastry (enough to wrap the beef)
- 1 egg, beaten

Instructions:

1. Preheat oven to 400°F (200°C).
2. Sear the beef tenderloin in olive oil in a hot pan for 2-3 minutes on each side until browned. Remove and let cool. Brush with mustard.
3. In a pan, melt butter and cook the mushrooms until they release their moisture and dry out. Add brandy, if using, and cook until the mixture is thick. Let cool.
4. Roll out puff pastry on a floured surface. Spread the mushroom mixture over the pastry and wrap the beef in it. Seal the edges.
5. Brush with beaten egg and bake for 30-35 minutes until golden. Let rest before serving.

Roast Beef and Yorkshire Pudding

For the Roast Beef:

- 3 lb (1.4kg) beef roast (such as rib-eye or sirloin)
- 2 tbsp olive oil
- 1 tbsp garlic powder
- 1 tbsp dried rosemary
- Salt and pepper to taste

For the Yorkshire Pudding:

- 1 cup (125g) all-purpose flour
- 1/2 tsp salt
- 3 large eggs
- 1 cup (240ml) whole milk
- 1 tbsp vegetable oil

Instructions:

1. Preheat oven to 375°F (190°C).
2. Rub the roast beef with olive oil, garlic powder, rosemary, salt, and pepper. Roast in the oven for 1.5-2 hours for medium rare, or until desired doneness is reached.
3. For the Yorkshire pudding: In a bowl, whisk together flour, salt, eggs, milk, and oil.
4. When the roast beef is done, remove it from the oven and let it rest. Pour the batter into a muffin tin or a shallow baking dish and bake for 20-25 minutes until puffed and golden.
5. Serve the roast beef with Yorkshire pudding and gravy.

Chicken Tikka Masala

Ingredients:

- 1 lb (450g) chicken breast, cubed
- 2 tbsp yogurt
- 1 tbsp ground turmeric
- 1 tbsp ground cumin
- 1 tbsp ground coriander
- 1 tbsp garam masala
- 2 tbsp vegetable oil
- 1 onion, chopped
- 2 cloves garlic, minced
- 1 can (14 oz/400g) diced tomatoes
- 1/2 cup (120ml) heavy cream
- Salt to taste

Instructions:

1. Marinate the chicken in yogurt, turmeric, cumin, coriander, garam masala, and a pinch of salt for 30 minutes.
2. Heat oil in a pan and cook the chicken until browned. Remove and set aside.
3. In the same pan, sauté onion and garlic until softened. Add diced tomatoes and cook for 10 minutes.
4. Add the chicken back to the pan and simmer for 10-15 minutes. Stir in heavy cream and cook until the sauce thickens.
5. Serve with rice or naan bread.

Bangers and Mash

Ingredients:

- 4 sausages (preferably pork sausages)
- 2 lbs (900g) potatoes, peeled and boiled
- 1/2 cup (120ml) milk
- 4 tbsp unsalted butter
- Salt and pepper to taste
- 1/4 cup (60ml) gravy (optional)

Instructions:

1. Grill or fry the sausages until browned and cooked through.
2. For the mash: Mash the boiled potatoes with milk, butter, salt, and pepper until smooth.
3. Serve the sausages on top of the mashed potatoes with gravy, if desired.

Toad in the Hole

Ingredients:

- 6 sausages
- 1 cup (125g) all-purpose flour
- 1/2 tsp salt
- 1 tsp baking powder
- 1 cup (240ml) milk
- 1 egg
- 2 tbsp vegetable oil

Instructions:

1. Preheat oven to 400°F (200°C).
2. Heat oil in a pan and brown the sausages for 5-7 minutes.
3. In a bowl, whisk flour, salt, baking powder, milk, and egg to form a batter.
4. Place the sausages in a baking dish and pour the batter over them.
5. Bake for 25-30 minutes until puffed and golden.

Beef Stew

Ingredients:

- 1 lb (450g) beef stew meat, cubed
- 2 tbsp vegetable oil
- 2 carrots, chopped
- 1 onion, chopped
- 2 cloves garlic, minced
- 1 cup (240ml) beef broth
- 1 cup (240ml) red wine
- 2 tbsp tomato paste
- 2 tsp dried thyme
- 1 tsp salt
- 1/2 tsp black pepper
- 2 tbsp flour

Instructions:

1. In a large pot, brown the beef stew meat in oil.
2. Add carrots, onion, and garlic, and cook until softened.
3. Stir in tomato paste, flour, thyme, salt, and pepper.
4. Add beef broth and red wine, bring to a boil, then simmer for 1.5-2 hours until the beef is tender.
5. Serve with bread or over mashed potatoes.

Chicken and Leek Pie

Ingredients:

- 2 chicken breasts, cooked and chopped
- 2 leeks, chopped
- 1/2 cup (120ml) chicken broth
- 1/2 cup (120ml) heavy cream
- 1 tbsp unsalted butter
- 1 tbsp all-purpose flour
- 1 package puff pastry
- 1 egg, beaten

Instructions:

1. In a pan, melt butter and cook leeks until soft. Stir in flour and cook for 1-2 minutes.
2. Add chicken broth and heavy cream, then bring to a simmer until thickened.
3. Stir in the cooked chicken and season with salt and pepper.
4. Roll out puff pastry and line a pie dish. Pour the filling into the dish.
5. Top with another layer of puff pastry, seal the edges, and brush with egg wash.
6. Bake at 375°F (190°C) for 25-30 minutes until golden.

Cornish Pasty

Ingredients:

- 2 cups (250g) all-purpose flour
- 1/2 tsp salt
- 1/2 cup (115g) unsalted butter, chilled
- 1/4 cup (60ml) cold water
- 1 lb (450g) beef, finely diced
- 1 potato, finely diced
- 1 onion, finely diced
- 1/4 cup (60g) turnip, finely diced
- Salt and pepper to taste

Instructions:

1. Preheat oven to 375°F (190°C) and grease a baking sheet.
2. For the dough: Combine flour and salt. Cut in butter until crumbly, then add cold water and knead into a dough.
3. Roll out dough and cut into circles.
4. Fill with beef, potato, onion, and turnip. Season with salt and pepper.
5. Fold the dough over to form a half-moon shape, sealing the edges.
6. Bake for 30-35 minutes until golden.

Steak and Kidney Pie

Ingredients:

- 1 lb (450g) beef steak, cubed
- 1/2 lb (225g) beef kidney, cubed
- 2 tbsp vegetable oil
- 1 onion, chopped
- 2 cloves garlic, minced
- 1 cup (240ml) beef broth
- 1/2 cup (120ml) red wine
- 1 tbsp tomato paste
- 1 tsp Worcestershire sauce
- 2 tbsp all-purpose flour
- 1 package puff pastry
- 1 egg, beaten

Instructions:

1. Brown steak and kidney in oil in a pan. Remove and set aside.
2. In the same pan, cook onion and garlic until soft. Stir in flour, tomato paste, Worcestershire sauce, broth, and wine.
3. Return the meat to the pan and simmer for 1-1.5 hours until tender.
4. Preheat oven to 375°F (190°C).
5. Roll out puff pastry and line a pie dish. Fill with meat mixture and top with pastry.
6. Seal the edges, brush with egg wash, and bake for 25-30 minutes.

Ploughman's Lunch

Ingredients:

- 2-3 slices of cheese (cheddar, stilton, or your favorite)
- 1-2 crusty bread rolls or slices of baguette
- 1 boiled egg, halved
- 1 small bunch of grapes or apple slices
- 1/4 cup (60g) pickled onions or chutney
- 1 handful of salad greens (lettuce, rocket, or spinach)
- 1 small portion of cold cuts (ham, roast beef, or turkey)

Instructions:

1. Arrange the cheese, bread, boiled egg, fruit, and cold cuts on a plate.
2. Serve with pickled onions or chutney and salad greens for a complete meal.

Full English Breakfast (served for dinner)

Ingredients:

- 2 sausages
- 2 slices of back bacon
- 2 eggs
- 2 small tomatoes, halved
- 1/2 cup (120g) baked beans
- 2 slices of black pudding (optional)
- 2 slices of buttered toast
- 1 tbsp vegetable oil for frying

Instructions:

1. Heat oil in a frying pan and cook sausages and bacon until browned and crispy.
2. In the same pan, fry the eggs to your liking and add the tomatoes, cut-side down, to grill for a few minutes.
3. Warm the baked beans in a small saucepan.
4. Fry black pudding in the pan until crispy (optional).
5. Serve with toast on the side. Enjoy with tea or coffee.

Lancashire Hotpot

Ingredients:

- 1 lb (450g) lamb shoulder, cubed
- 2 tbsp vegetable oil
- 2 medium onions, sliced
- 2 carrots, sliced
- 4 medium potatoes, peeled and sliced thinly
- 1/2 cup (120ml) beef or lamb broth
- 1 tsp dried thyme
- Salt and pepper to taste

Instructions:

1. Preheat oven to 350°F (175°C).
2. In a pan, brown the lamb cubes in vegetable oil. Remove and set aside.
3. In the same pan, sauté onions and carrots until softened.
4. In a casserole dish, layer the lamb, vegetables, and sliced potatoes. Season with thyme, salt, and pepper.
5. Pour the broth over the mixture and cover with foil.
6. Bake for 1.5-2 hours, removing the foil for the last 20 minutes to brown the potatoes.

Beef and Ale Stew

Ingredients:

- 1 lb (450g) beef stew meat, cubed
- 2 tbsp vegetable oil
- 2 medium onions, chopped
- 2 cloves garlic, minced
- 2 carrots, chopped
- 1 cup (240ml) ale (preferably stout or brown ale)
- 2 cups (480ml) beef broth
- 1 tbsp tomato paste
- 1 tsp dried thyme
- Salt and pepper to taste

Instructions:

1. Heat oil in a pan and brown the beef cubes. Remove and set aside.
2. In the same pan, cook onions and garlic until softened.
3. Stir in tomato paste, thyme, and vegetables, and cook for another 2 minutes.
4. Pour in the ale and beef broth, scraping the bottom of the pan.
5. Return beef to the pan, season with salt and pepper, and simmer for 1.5-2 hours, until beef is tender.

Spaghetti Bolognese (British-style)

Ingredients:

- 1 lb (450g) ground beef or pork
- 1 medium onion, chopped
- 2 cloves garlic, minced
- 1 can (14 oz/400g) diced tomatoes
- 1/4 cup (60ml) red wine (optional)
- 1 tbsp tomato paste
- 1 tsp dried oregano
- 1/2 tsp dried basil
- 1 tbsp olive oil
- 8 oz (225g) spaghetti

Instructions:

1. Heat oil in a pan and brown the ground meat. Add onions and garlic and cook until softened.
2. Stir in the tomato paste, diced tomatoes, wine (if using), oregano, and basil.
3. Simmer for 30 minutes until the sauce thickens.
4. Cook spaghetti according to package instructions and serve with the Bolognese sauce on top.

Fish Pie

Ingredients:

- 1 lb (450g) white fish fillets (cod, haddock, or pollock), cut into chunks
- 1/2 lb (225g) shrimp, peeled
- 3 cups (720ml) milk
- 2 tbsp unsalted butter
- 2 tbsp all-purpose flour
- 1/4 tsp ground nutmeg
- 1/4 cup (60g) frozen peas
- 2 tbsp fresh parsley, chopped
- 4 large potatoes, peeled and boiled
- Salt and pepper to taste

Instructions:

1. Preheat oven to 375°F (190°C) and grease a baking dish.
2. In a saucepan, melt butter and stir in flour to create a roux. Gradually add milk while whisking. Cook for 5-7 minutes until thickened.
3. Stir in nutmeg, peas, parsley, and season with salt and pepper.
4. Add fish and shrimp to the sauce and cook for 5 minutes until just cooked.
5. Mash the boiled potatoes with butter and season with salt and pepper.
6. Pour the fish mixture into the baking dish, top with mashed potatoes, and bake for 20-25 minutes until golden.

Sausage Rolls

Ingredients:

- 1 lb (450g) sausage meat
- 1 package puff pastry
- 1 egg, beaten

Instructions:

1. Preheat oven to 375°F (190°C) and line a baking sheet with parchment paper.
2. Roll out puff pastry and cut into rectangles.
3. Place a line of sausage meat along the center of each rectangle, then fold the pastry over the meat and seal the edges.
4. Brush with beaten egg and bake for 20-25 minutes until golden and cooked through.

Ragu

Ingredients:

- 1 lb (450g) ground beef or pork
- 1 medium onion, chopped
- 2 cloves garlic, minced
- 2 carrots, chopped
- 1 can (14 oz/400g) diced tomatoes
- 1/4 cup (60ml) red wine (optional)
- 1 tbsp tomato paste
- 1 tsp dried oregano
- 1/2 tsp dried basil
- Salt and pepper to taste

Instructions:

1. In a pan, cook ground meat until browned. Add onions and garlic and cook until softened.
2. Stir in tomato paste, diced tomatoes, wine (if using), oregano, basil, and season with salt and pepper.
3. Simmer for 30-40 minutes until the sauce thickens.
4. Serve over pasta or as a filling for sandwiches.

Lamb Chops with Mint Sauce

Ingredients:

- 4 lamb chops
- 2 tbsp olive oil
- 1 tbsp fresh rosemary, chopped
- 2 cloves garlic, minced
- 1/4 cup (60ml) white wine (optional)
- Salt and pepper to taste

For the mint sauce:

- 1/4 cup (60ml) white wine vinegar
- 2 tbsp fresh mint, chopped
- 1 tbsp sugar

Instructions:

1. Preheat grill or pan over medium heat.
2. Season lamb chops with olive oil, rosemary, garlic, salt, and pepper.
3. Cook lamb chops for 3-4 minutes per side until browned and cooked to your preferred doneness.
4. For the mint sauce: Mix vinegar, mint, and sugar in a bowl. Stir to dissolve the sugar.
5. Serve the lamb chops with mint sauce on the side.

Chicken Casserole

Ingredients:

- 4 chicken thighs (bone-in, skin-on)
- 1 onion, chopped
- 2 cloves garlic, minced
- 2 carrots, chopped
- 2 cups (480ml) chicken broth
- 1/2 cup (120ml) white wine (optional)
- 1 tbsp fresh thyme, chopped
- Salt and pepper to taste
- 1 tbsp olive oil

Instructions:

1. Preheat oven to 375°F (190°C).
2. Heat olive oil in a pan and brown the chicken thighs on both sides. Remove and set aside.
3. In the same pan, cook onion, garlic, and carrots until softened.
4. Stir in chicken broth, wine (if using), thyme, and season with salt and pepper.
5. Return chicken to the pan, cover, and bake for 45-50 minutes until the chicken is cooked through.

Cauliflower Cheese

Ingredients:

- 1 large cauliflower, cut into florets
- 2 tbsp unsalted butter
- 2 tbsp all-purpose flour
- 2 cups (480ml) milk
- 1 1/2 cups (180g) sharp cheddar cheese, grated
- Salt and pepper to taste

Instructions:

1. Preheat oven to 375°F (190°C) and grease a baking dish.
2. Steam the cauliflower florets until tender, then place them in the baking dish.
3. In a saucepan, melt butter and stir in flour to make a roux. Gradually add milk while whisking until thickened.
4. Stir in cheese and season with salt and pepper.
5. Pour the cheese sauce over the cauliflower and bake for 20-25 minutes until bubbly and golden.

Sunday Roast

Ingredients:

For the roast:

- 3 lb (1.4kg) beef, lamb, or chicken
- 2 tbsp olive oil
- 1 tbsp fresh rosemary, chopped
- 1 tbsp fresh thyme, chopped
- Salt and pepper to taste

For the sides:

- 4 large potatoes, peeled and cut into chunks
- 1 lb (450g) carrots, peeled
- 1/2 lb (225g) Brussels sprouts, trimmed

Instructions:

1. Preheat oven to 375°F (190°C).
2. Season the roast with olive oil, rosemary, thyme, salt, and pepper. Roast for 1.5-2 hours, depending on the type and size of the meat.
3. Roast potatoes, carrots, and Brussels sprouts in a separate pan for 45-50 minutes, tossing halfway through.
4. Serve the roast with the vegetables and gravy.

Black Pudding and Eggs

Ingredients:

- 2 slices of black pudding
- 2 eggs
- 1 tbsp vegetable oil
- Salt and pepper to taste

Instructions:

1. Heat oil in a frying pan over medium heat.
2. Fry black pudding slices for 3-4 minutes per side until crispy and golden. Remove and set aside.
3. In the same pan, fry the eggs to your liking (fried, scrambled, or poached).
4. Serve the black pudding alongside the eggs with toast or fried potatoes.

Pork Pie

Ingredients:

For the filling:

- 1 lb (450g) ground pork
- 1/4 lb (115g) pork fat, diced
- 1 tbsp fresh sage, chopped
- 1/2 tsp ground white pepper
- Salt to taste
- 1/4 cup (60ml) chicken stock

For the pastry:

- 2 cups (250g) all-purpose flour
- 1/2 tsp salt
- 1/4 cup (60g) lard, chilled
- 1/4 cup (60g) unsalted butter, chilled
- 1/4 cup (60ml) cold water

Instructions:

1. Preheat oven to 375°F (190°C) and grease a pie pan.
2. For the pastry: Combine flour and salt. Cut in the lard and butter until crumbly. Add cold water and mix until the dough comes together.
3. Roll out the dough and line the pie pan with it.
4. For the filling: Mix ground pork, pork fat, sage, pepper, salt, and chicken stock in a bowl.
5. Fill the pie shell with the pork mixture, then cover with another layer of pastry. Seal the edges and cut a small hole in the center.
6. Bake for 45-50 minutes until golden.

Scampi and Chips

Ingredients:

- 12-16 large scampi (or prawns)
- 1 cup (125g) all-purpose flour
- 1/2 cup (120ml) cold beer or sparkling water
- 1/2 tsp salt
- Vegetable oil (for frying)
- 4 medium potatoes, peeled and cut into chips (fries)
- Salt to taste

Instructions:

1. Heat oil in a deep fryer or pan to 350°F (175°C).
2. For the chips: Fry the potato chips in batches for 4-5 minutes until soft but not golden. Remove and set aside.
3. For the scampi: In a bowl, whisk together flour, salt, and beer or sparkling water to make a batter.
4. Dip scampi into the batter and fry for 3-4 minutes until golden and crispy.
5. Fry the chips again for 3-4 minutes until golden and crispy.
6. Serve the scampi with the chips, lemon wedges, and tartar sauce.

Welsh Rarebit

Ingredients:

- 2 slices of bread (preferably thick-cut white bread)
- 1 cup (120g) sharp cheddar cheese, grated
- 1 tbsp unsalted butter
- 1 tbsp all-purpose flour
- 1/2 cup (120ml) milk
- 1 tsp Worcestershire sauce
- 1/2 tsp Dijon mustard
- 1 egg yolk
- Salt and pepper to taste

Instructions:

1. Preheat the grill or broiler.
2. Toast the bread slices until lightly browned and crispy.
3. In a saucepan, melt butter and stir in flour to make a roux. Gradually add milk while whisking until smooth.
4. Stir in cheese, Worcestershire sauce, mustard, egg yolk, and season with salt and pepper.
5. Pour the cheese mixture over the toasted bread and grill for 3-4 minutes until bubbling and golden.

Scotch Eggs

Ingredients:

- 4 hard-boiled eggs
- 1 lb (450g) sausage meat
- 1/4 cup (30g) breadcrumbs
- 1/2 cup (60g) flour
- 1 large egg, beaten
- Vegetable oil (for frying)

Instructions:

1. Peel the hard-boiled eggs.
2. In a bowl, shape the sausage meat into thin patties.
3. Wrap each egg with sausage meat and roll in flour.
4. Dip in beaten egg, then coat with breadcrumbs.
5. Heat oil in a deep fryer or pan to 350°F (175°C) and fry the Scotch eggs for 4-5 minutes until golden and cooked through.
6. Serve warm or cold with mustard.

Sausage and Onion Casserole

Ingredients:

- 6 sausages (preferably pork)
- 2 large onions, sliced
- 2 cloves garlic, minced
- 1 cup (240ml) beef broth
- 1 tbsp Worcestershire sauce
- 1 tbsp tomato paste
- 1 tbsp fresh thyme, chopped
- Salt and pepper to taste
- 2 tbsp olive oil

Instructions:

1. Preheat oven to 375°F (190°C).
2. Heat olive oil in a pan and brown the sausages. Remove and set aside.
3. In the same pan, sauté onions and garlic until softened.
4. Stir in tomato paste, Worcestershire sauce, thyme, beef broth, and season with salt and pepper.
5. Add the sausages back into the pan and transfer to the oven.
6. Bake for 30-40 minutes until the sausages are cooked through and the sauce thickens.

Grilled Kippers

Ingredients:

- 2 kipper fillets (smoked herring)
- 1 tbsp olive oil
- 1 tbsp lemon juice
- Salt and pepper to taste

Instructions:

1. Preheat grill or broiler.
2. Rub kipper fillets with olive oil, lemon juice, salt, and pepper.
3. Grill for 4-5 minutes per side until heated through and slightly crispy.
4. Serve with toast and butter.

Bubble and Squeak

Ingredients:

- 4 large potatoes, boiled and mashed
- 2 cups (300g) cooked cabbage, chopped
- 1 small onion, chopped
- 2 tbsp vegetable oil
- Salt and pepper to taste

Instructions:

1. In a frying pan, heat oil and sauté onions until softened.
2. Add the mashed potatoes and cooked cabbage, stirring to combine.
3. Press the mixture into the pan and cook over medium heat for 5-7 minutes until crispy on the bottom.
4. Flip and cook for another 5 minutes until both sides are golden and crispy.
5. Serve as a side dish or with a fried egg on top.

Moussaka (British Adaptation)

Ingredients:

- 2 medium aubergines (eggplant), sliced
- 1 lb (450g) ground lamb or beef
- 1 onion, chopped
- 2 cloves garlic, minced
- 1 can (14 oz/400g) diced tomatoes
- 1 tbsp tomato paste
- 1 tsp ground cinnamon
- 1/2 tsp ground nutmeg
- 1/4 cup (60ml) red wine (optional)
- 2 tbsp olive oil
- 1/4 cup (30g) grated Parmesan cheese

For the Bechamel Sauce:

- 2 tbsp unsalted butter
- 2 tbsp all-purpose flour
- 2 cups (480ml) milk
- 1/2 cup (60g) grated cheddar cheese
- Salt and pepper to taste

Instructions:

1. Preheat oven to 375°F (190°C).
2. Fry the eggplant slices in olive oil until browned, then set aside.
3. In a pan, cook the ground meat with onion and garlic until browned. Stir in diced tomatoes, tomato paste, cinnamon, nutmeg, and wine. Simmer for 20 minutes.
4. For the bechamel sauce: Melt butter in a saucepan, stir in flour, and gradually add milk while whisking until thickened. Stir in cheese, then season with salt and pepper.
5. In a baking dish, layer eggplant slices, meat sauce, and bechamel sauce. Repeat the layers and top with Parmesan.
6. Bake for 30-35 minutes until golden and bubbling.

Chilli Con Carne

Ingredients:

- 1 lb (450g) ground beef
- 1 onion, chopped
- 2 cloves garlic, minced
- 1 can (14 oz/400g) diced tomatoes
- 1 can (14 oz/400g) kidney beans, drained and rinsed
- 1 tbsp chili powder
- 1 tsp ground cumin
- 1 tsp smoked paprika
- Salt and pepper to taste

Instructions:

1. In a pan, cook the ground beef with onion and garlic until browned.
2. Add tomatoes, kidney beans, chili powder, cumin, paprika, salt, and pepper.
3. Simmer for 20-30 minutes until thickened.
4. Serve with rice, tortilla chips, or cornbread.

Hot Pot

Ingredients:

- 1 lb (450g) lamb or beef, cubed
- 2 medium onions, chopped
- 2 cloves garlic, minced
- 4 medium potatoes, sliced thinly
- 2 carrots, sliced
- 1 cup (240ml) beef broth
- 1 tbsp Worcestershire sauce
- 1 tbsp fresh thyme, chopped
- Salt and pepper to taste

Instructions:

1. Preheat oven to 375°F (190°C).
2. Brown the lamb or beef in a pan, then remove and set aside.
3. In the same pan, sauté onions and garlic until softened.
4. In a baking dish, layer the meat, onions, garlic, potatoes, and carrots.
5. Pour over beef broth and Worcestershire sauce, season with thyme, salt, and pepper.
6. Cover with foil and bake for 1.5 hours, removing the foil for the last 30 minutes.

Venison Stew

Ingredients:

- 1 lb (450g) venison stew meat
- 2 tbsp vegetable oil
- 2 onions, chopped
- 2 carrots, chopped
- 2 cloves garlic, minced
- 1 cup (240ml) red wine
- 2 cups (480ml) beef broth
- 1 tbsp fresh rosemary, chopped
- 1 tsp dried thyme
- Salt and pepper to taste

Instructions:

1. In a pan, brown the venison stew meat in vegetable oil. Remove and set aside.
2. Sauté onions, carrots, and garlic in the same pan until softened.
3. Stir in red wine and cook for 2 minutes, scraping the pan.
4. Add beef broth, rosemary, thyme, venison, and season with salt and pepper.
5. Simmer for 1.5-2 hours until the venison is tender.

Roast Chicken with Stuffing

Ingredients:

For the chicken:

- 1 whole chicken (about 4 lbs/1.8 kg)
- 2 tbsp olive oil
- 1 tbsp fresh rosemary, chopped
- 1 tbsp fresh thyme, chopped
- Salt and pepper to taste
- 1 lemon, halved
- 4 garlic cloves, smashed

For the stuffing:

- 1 cup (125g) breadcrumbs
- 1/4 cup (60g) unsalted butter, melted
- 1/2 cup (120ml) chicken broth
- 1 small onion, chopped
- 1 celery stalk, chopped
- 1/2 tsp dried sage
- Salt and pepper to taste

Instructions:

1. Preheat oven to 375°F (190°C).
2. For the stuffing: Sauté the onion and celery in melted butter until soft. Stir in breadcrumbs, sage, and chicken broth. Season with salt and pepper.
3. Stuff the chicken with the mixture and place it in a roasting pan.
4. Rub olive oil, rosemary, thyme, salt, and pepper all over the chicken. Insert lemon halves and garlic cloves inside the cavity of the chicken.
5. Roast the chicken for 1.5-2 hours, basting occasionally, until the internal temperature reaches 165°F (74°C).
6. Serve with roasted vegetables and gravy.

Steak and Chips

Ingredients:

- 2 rib-eye steaks (or your preferred cut)
- 2 tbsp olive oil
- Salt and pepper to taste
- 4 large potatoes, peeled and cut into thick chips (fries)
- 1 tbsp vegetable oil (for frying)

Instructions:

1. Preheat oven to 400°F (200°C).
2. For the chips: Heat vegetable oil in a frying pan. Fry the chips for 4-5 minutes until soft but not golden. Remove and set aside.
3. Bake the chips in the oven for 25-30 minutes until golden and crispy.
4. Heat olive oil in a pan over medium-high heat. Season the steaks with salt and pepper, then fry for 4-5 minutes per side for medium-rare, or longer for desired doneness.
5. Serve the steaks with chips and your choice of sauce (peppercorn or béarnaise).

Gammon and Eggs

Ingredients:

- 2 gammon steaks (about 6 oz/170g each)
- 2 eggs
- 1 tbsp vegetable oil
- Salt and pepper to taste

Instructions:

1. Heat the oil in a frying pan over medium heat.
2. Fry the gammon steaks for 5-7 minutes on each side until golden and cooked through.
3. In a separate pan, fry the eggs to your liking (fried, poached, or scrambled).
4. Serve the gammon steaks with the fried eggs on top and a side of chips or peas.

Toad in the Hole with Gravy

Ingredients:

For the batter:

- 1 cup (125g) all-purpose flour
- 1/2 tsp salt
- 1 tsp baking powder
- 1 cup (240ml) milk
- 1 egg

For the sausages and gravy:

- 6 sausages (preferably pork)
- 2 tbsp vegetable oil
- 2 tbsp all-purpose flour
- 2 cups (480ml) beef or chicken broth
- 1 tsp Worcestershire sauce
- Salt and pepper to taste

Instructions:

1. Preheat oven to 400°F (200°C).
2. Heat oil in a pan and brown the sausages on all sides. Remove and set aside.
3. For the batter: In a bowl, whisk together flour, salt, baking powder, milk, and egg to make a smooth batter.
4. Pour the batter into a greased baking dish and place the browned sausages in the batter.
5. Bake for 25-30 minutes until the batter is puffed and golden.
6. For the gravy: In the same pan, whisk flour into the remaining fat from the sausages. Gradually add broth and Worcestershire sauce, then bring to a simmer until thickened.
7. Serve the toad in the hole with gravy.

Pork Roast with Apple Sauce

Ingredients:

- 1.5-2 lb (700g-900g) pork loin roast
- 2 tbsp olive oil
- 1 tbsp fresh rosemary, chopped
- Salt and pepper to taste
- 2 apples, peeled and chopped
- 1/4 cup (60ml) water
- 1 tbsp brown sugar

Instructions:

1. Preheat oven to 375°F (190°C).
2. Rub pork roast with olive oil, rosemary, salt, and pepper.
3. Place the roast on a rack in a roasting pan and roast for 1-1.5 hours, basting occasionally, until the internal temperature reaches 145°F (63°C).
4. For the apple sauce: In a saucepan, combine apples, water, and brown sugar. Simmer for 10-15 minutes until apples are soft and the sauce thickens.
5. Serve the pork roast with apple sauce on the side.

Prawn Cocktail (Starter but often part of a dinner)

Ingredients:

- 12-16 large cooked prawns (shrimp), peeled and deveined
- 1/4 cup (60ml) mayonnaise
- 2 tbsp ketchup
- 1 tbsp fresh lemon juice
- 1 tsp Worcestershire sauce
- 1 tsp brandy (optional)
- A few lettuce leaves, shredded
- Lemon wedges for garnish

Instructions:

1. In a bowl, mix mayonnaise, ketchup, lemon juice, Worcestershire sauce, and brandy (if using) to make the cocktail sauce.
2. Place shredded lettuce in serving glasses or bowls.
3. Arrange prawns on top and spoon the cocktail sauce over the prawns.
4. Garnish with lemon wedges and serve chilled.

Chicken Pot Pie

Ingredients:

For the filling:

- 2 cups (300g) cooked chicken, shredded
- 1 cup (150g) carrots, diced
- 1 cup (150g) peas
- 1 medium onion, chopped
- 2 cloves garlic, minced
- 2 tbsp unsalted butter
- 2 tbsp all-purpose flour
- 2 cups (480ml) chicken broth
- 1/2 cup (120ml) heavy cream
- Salt and pepper to taste

For the crust:

- 1 package puff pastry or pie dough

Instructions:

1. Preheat oven to 375°F (190°C).
2. In a pan, melt butter and sauté onions and garlic until softened. Stir in flour and cook for 1-2 minutes.
3. Gradually add chicken broth and heavy cream, whisking until thickened.
4. Stir in the cooked chicken, carrots, and peas, then season with salt and pepper.
5. Pour the filling into a greased baking dish.
6. Roll out the puff pastry or pie dough and place it over the filling, trimming any excess. Cut slits in the top to allow steam to escape.
7. Bake for 25-30 minutes, or until golden and bubbly.

Lamb Shanks with Rosemary

Ingredients:

- 2 lamb shanks
- 2 tbsp olive oil
- 1 medium onion, chopped
- 2 cloves garlic, minced
- 1 cup (240ml) red wine
- 2 cups (480ml) beef or lamb broth
- 2 tbsp fresh rosemary, chopped
- 1 tsp dried thyme
- Salt and pepper to taste

Instructions:

1. Preheat oven to 350°F (175°C).
2. Heat olive oil in a heavy ovenproof pot and brown the lamb shanks on all sides. Remove and set aside.
3. In the same pot, sauté onion and garlic until softened.
4. Add red wine and simmer for 5 minutes.
5. Add broth, rosemary, thyme, and season with salt and pepper. Return the lamb shanks to the pot.
6. Cover and cook in the oven for 1.5-2 hours, until the lamb is tender and falling off the bone.

Shepherd's Pie with Sweet Potato Topping

Ingredients:

For the filling:

- 1 lb (450g) ground lamb
- 1 medium onion, chopped
- 2 cloves garlic, minced
- 2 carrots, diced
- 1 cup (240ml) beef broth
- 1 tbsp tomato paste
- 1 tsp Worcestershire sauce
- 1 tbsp fresh thyme, chopped
- Salt and pepper to taste

For the topping:

- 3 medium sweet potatoes, peeled and chopped
- 2 tbsp unsalted butter
- 1/4 cup (60ml) milk
- Salt and pepper to taste

Instructions:

1. Preheat oven to 375°F (190°C).
2. For the filling: Brown the ground lamb in a pan, then add onion, garlic, and carrots, and cook until softened.
3. Stir in tomato paste, Worcestershire sauce, thyme, and beef broth. Simmer for 15 minutes until thickened.
4. For the topping: Boil the sweet potatoes until tender. Drain and mash with butter, milk, salt, and pepper.
5. Transfer the lamb mixture to a baking dish, top with mashed sweet potatoes, and spread evenly.
6. Bake for 20-25 minutes until golden.

Chicken and Mushroom Pie

Ingredients:

For the filling:

- 2 cups (300g) cooked chicken, shredded
- 1 cup (150g) mushrooms, sliced
- 1 medium onion, chopped
- 2 cloves garlic, minced
- 2 tbsp unsalted butter
- 2 tbsp all-purpose flour
- 2 cups (480ml) chicken broth
- 1/2 cup (120ml) heavy cream
- Salt and pepper to taste

For the crust:

- 1 package puff pastry or pie dough

Instructions:

1. Preheat oven to 375°F (190°C).
2. In a pan, melt butter and sauté onions, garlic, and mushrooms until softened. Stir in flour and cook for 1-2 minutes.
3. Gradually add chicken broth and heavy cream, whisking until thickened.
4. Stir in the cooked chicken, and season with salt and pepper.
5. Pour the filling into a greased baking dish.
6. Roll out puff pastry or pie dough and place it over the filling. Trim the excess and cut slits in the top.
7. Bake for 25-30 minutes, or until golden and bubbling.

Chicken Fricassée

Ingredients:

- 4 chicken thighs (bone-in, skin-on)
- 2 tbsp olive oil
- 1 medium onion, chopped
- 2 cloves garlic, minced
- 2 carrots, chopped
- 1 cup (240ml) chicken broth
- 1/2 cup (120ml) white wine
- 1/2 cup (120ml) heavy cream
- 1 tbsp fresh thyme, chopped
- Salt and pepper to taste

Instructions:

1. Heat olive oil in a pan over medium heat and brown the chicken thighs on both sides. Remove and set aside.
2. In the same pan, sauté onion, garlic, and carrots until softened.
3. Add white wine and chicken broth, then return the chicken to the pan.
4. Simmer for 30-40 minutes until the chicken is cooked through.
5. Stir in heavy cream and thyme, and cook for another 5 minutes.
6. Season with salt and pepper to taste and serve with rice or mashed potatoes.

Korma Curry (British-style)

Ingredients:

- 1 lb (450g) chicken breast, cubed
- 1 tbsp vegetable oil
- 1 medium onion, chopped
- 2 cloves garlic, minced
- 1 tbsp ginger, grated
- 2 tbsp korma curry paste
- 1 can (14 oz/400g) coconut milk
- 1/4 cup (60g) ground almonds
- 1 tbsp fresh coriander, chopped (optional)
- Salt to taste

Instructions:

1. Heat oil in a pan and sauté onion, garlic, and ginger until softened.
2. Stir in korma curry paste and cook for 2 minutes.
3. Add chicken and cook until browned.
4. Pour in coconut milk and ground almonds, then simmer for 15-20 minutes until thickened.
5. Garnish with fresh coriander and serve with basmati rice.

Faggots and Peas

Ingredients:

For the faggots:

- 1 lb (450g) ground pork
- 1/2 lb (225g) pork liver, finely chopped
- 1/2 cup (60g) breadcrumbs
- 1/4 cup (60ml) chicken broth
- 1 onion, chopped
- 1 tbsp fresh parsley, chopped
- Salt and pepper to taste

For the peas:

- 2 cups (240g) peas (fresh or frozen)
- 1 tbsp butter
- Salt and pepper to taste

Instructions:

1. Preheat oven to 350°F (175°C).
2. For the faggots: Mix ground pork, pork liver, breadcrumbs, chicken broth, onion, parsley, salt, and pepper. Shape into small meatballs.
3. Place the faggots in a baking dish and bake for 30-40 minutes until cooked through.
4. For the peas: Cook the peas in boiling water for 3-4 minutes, then drain and toss with butter, salt, and pepper.
5. Serve the faggots with peas and gravy.

Grilled Mackerel

Ingredients:

- 2 mackerel fillets
- 1 tbsp olive oil
- 1 tbsp lemon juice
- Salt and pepper to taste

Instructions:

1. Preheat grill or broiler.
2. Rub the mackerel fillets with olive oil, lemon juice, salt, and pepper.
3. Grill the fillets for 4-5 minutes on each side until cooked through.
4. Serve with a side of roasted vegetables or salad.